Where W

by Wiley Blevins • illustrated by Kyle Poling

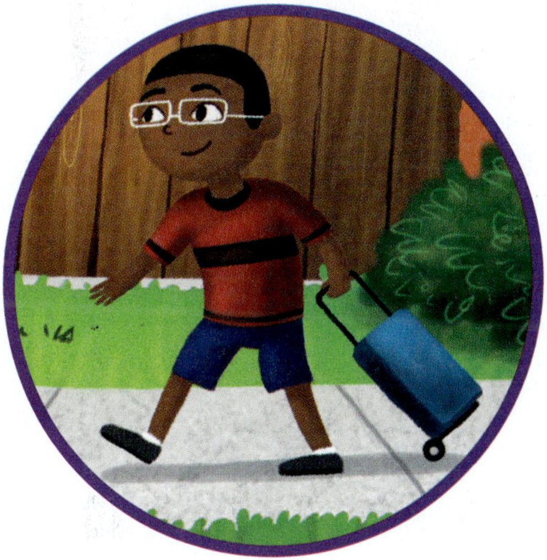

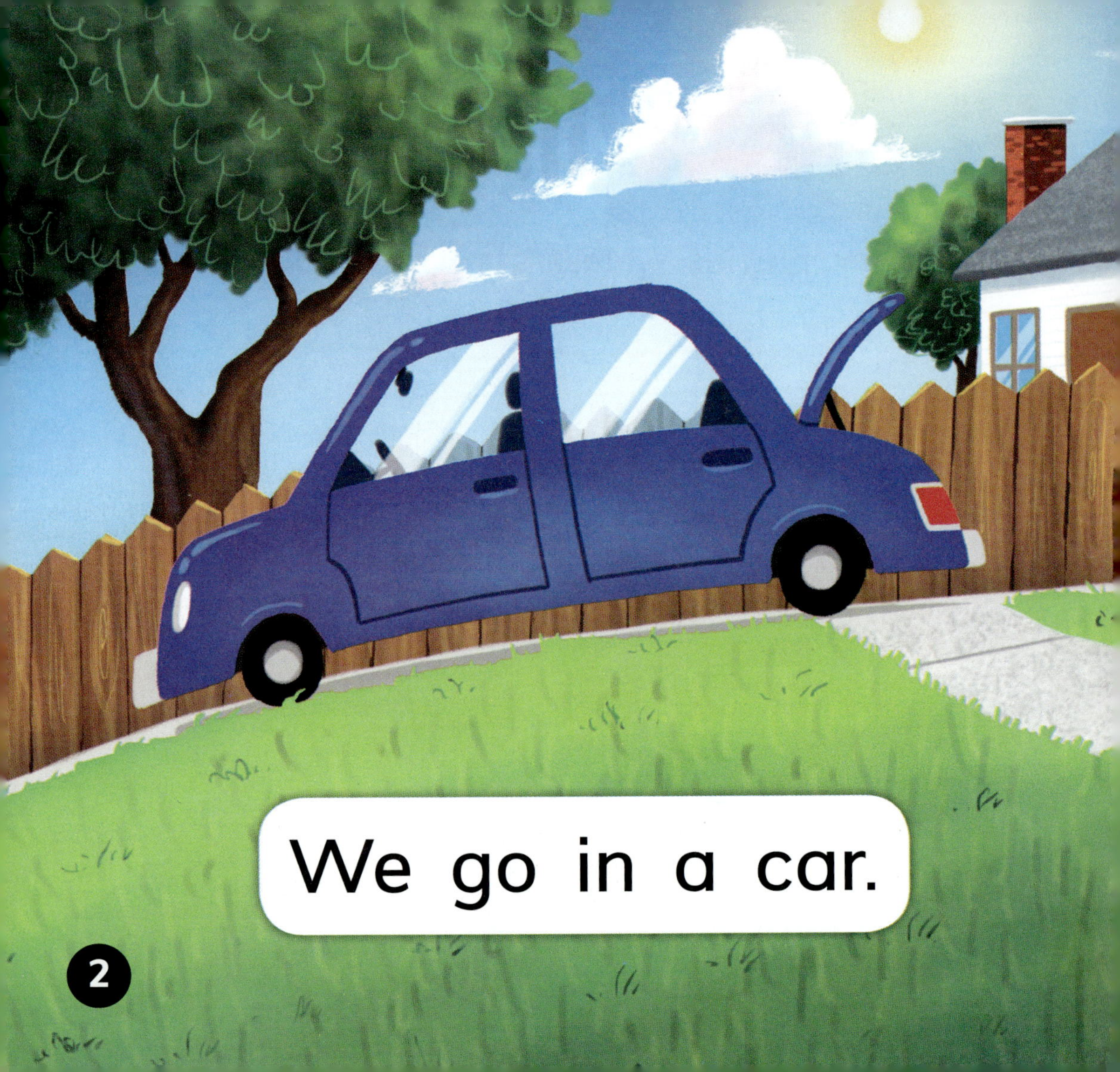

We go in a car.

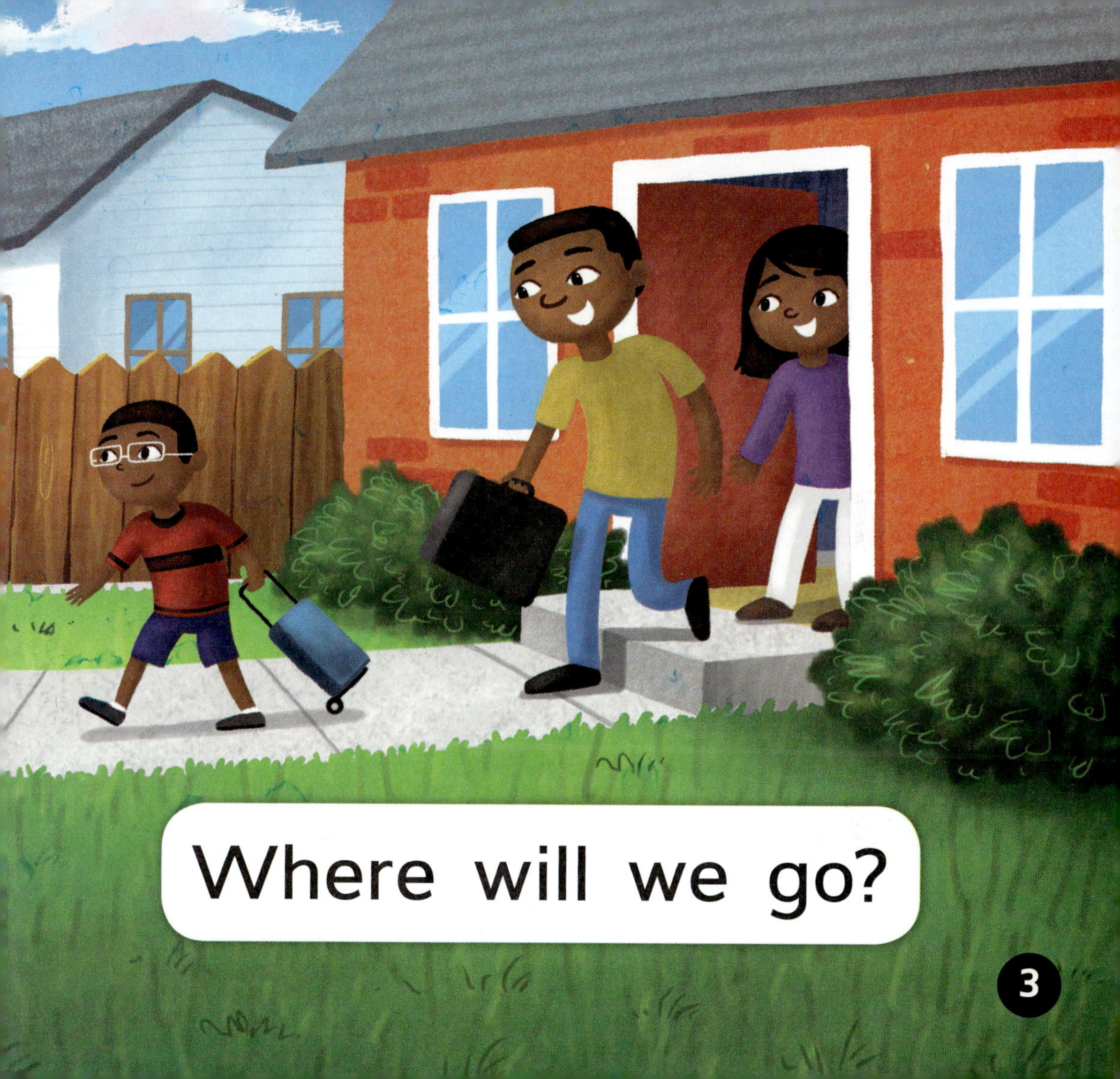

Where will we go?

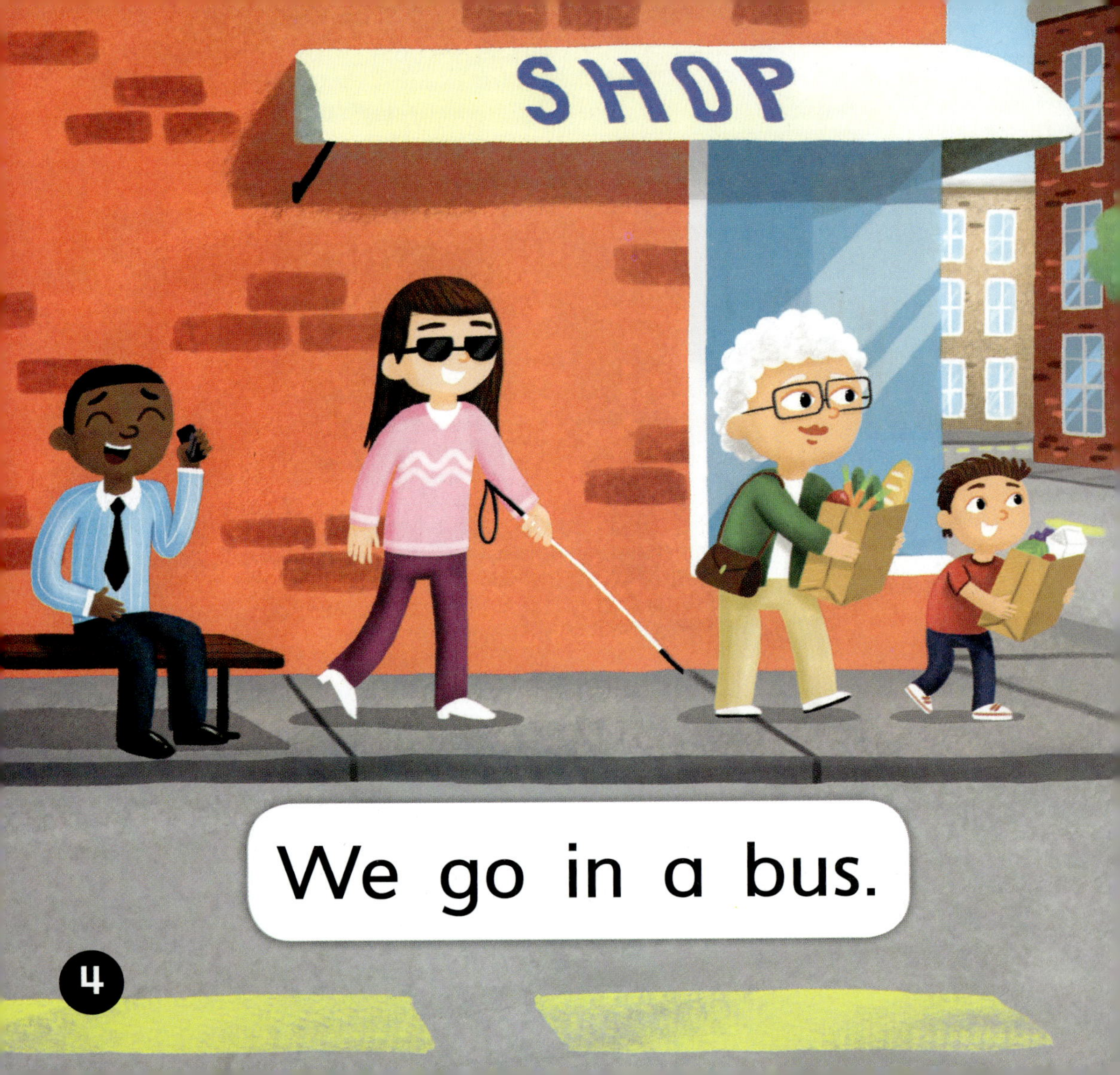

We go in a bus.

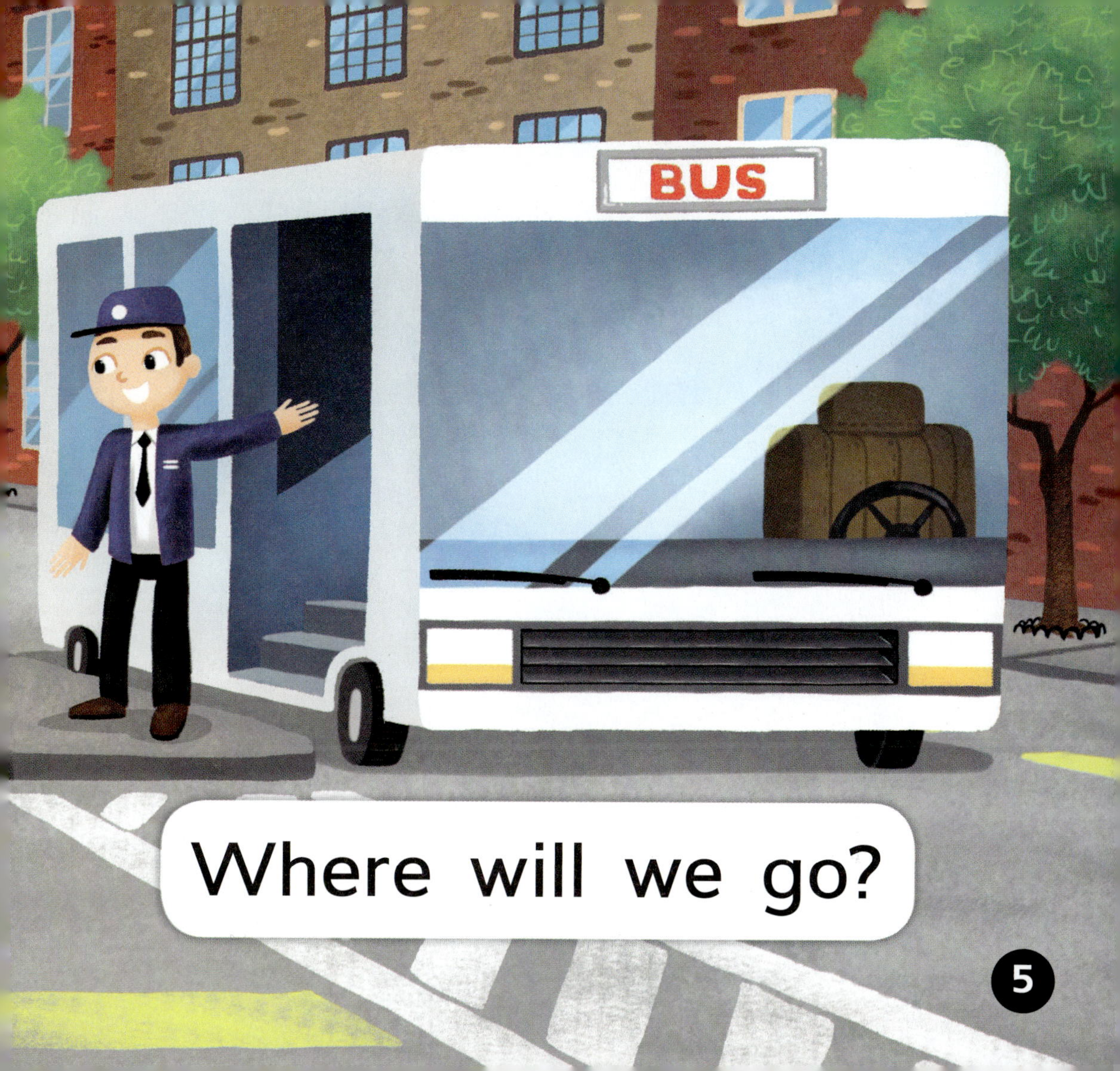

Where will we go?

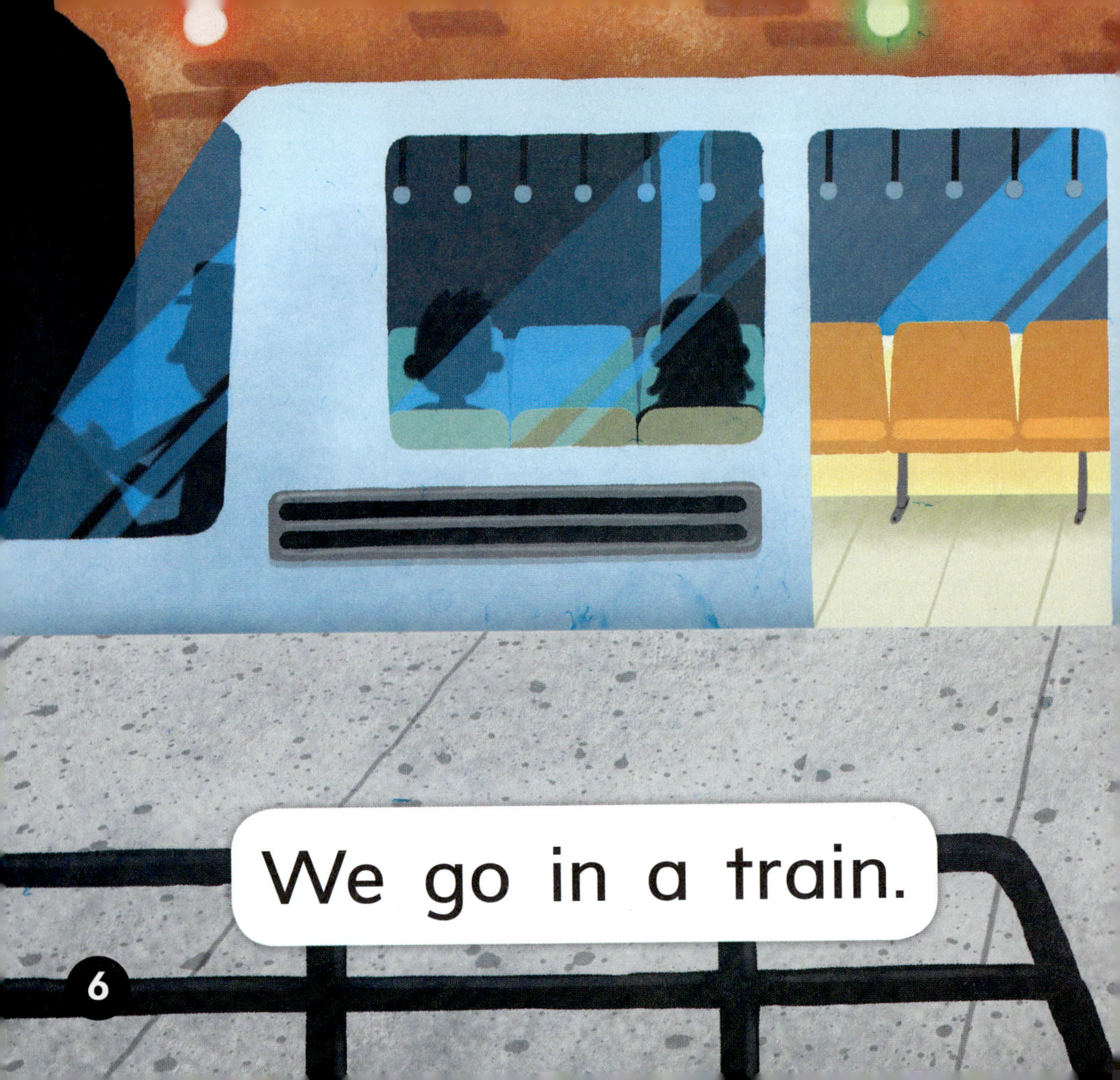

We go in a train.

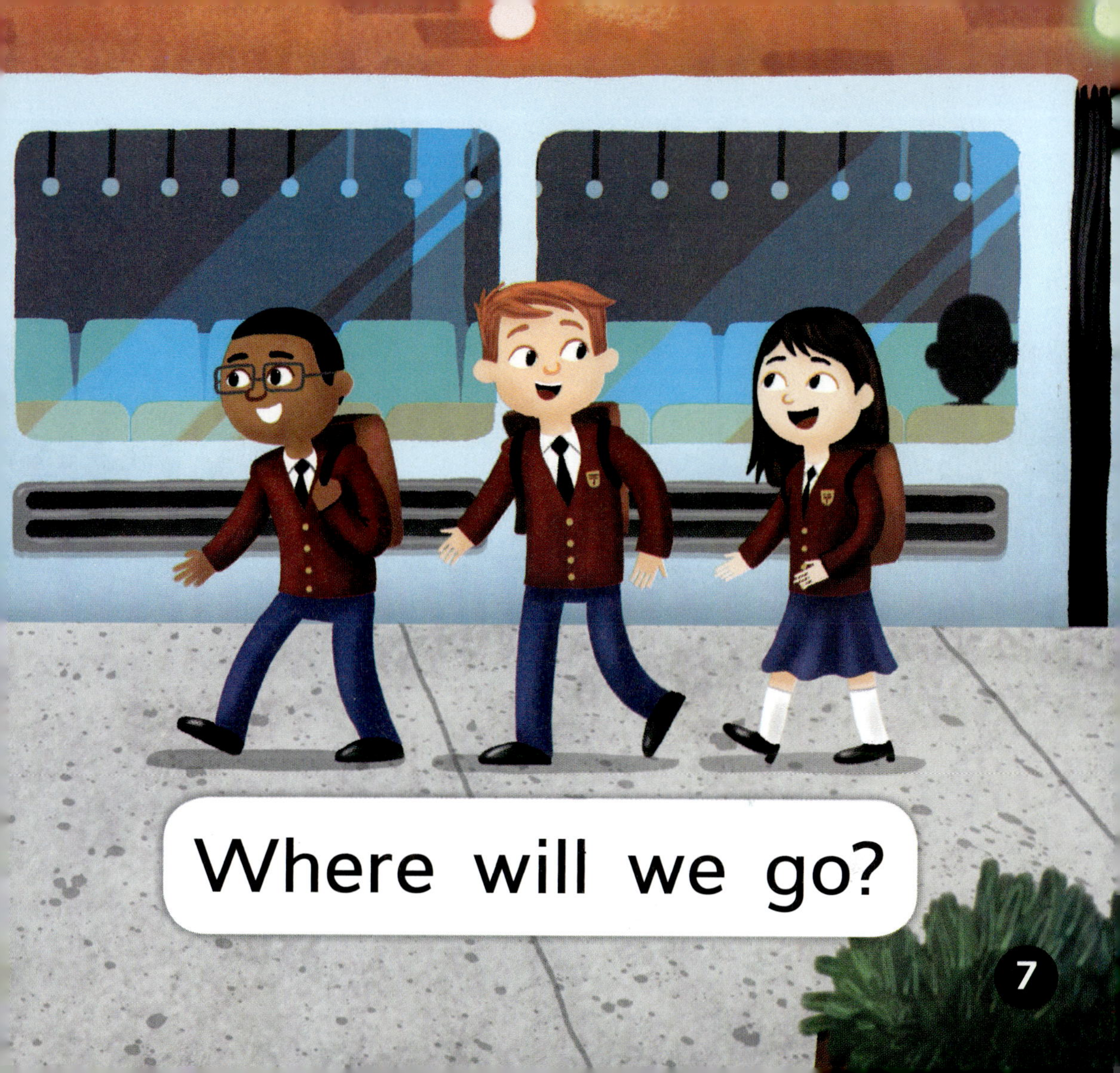

Where will we go?

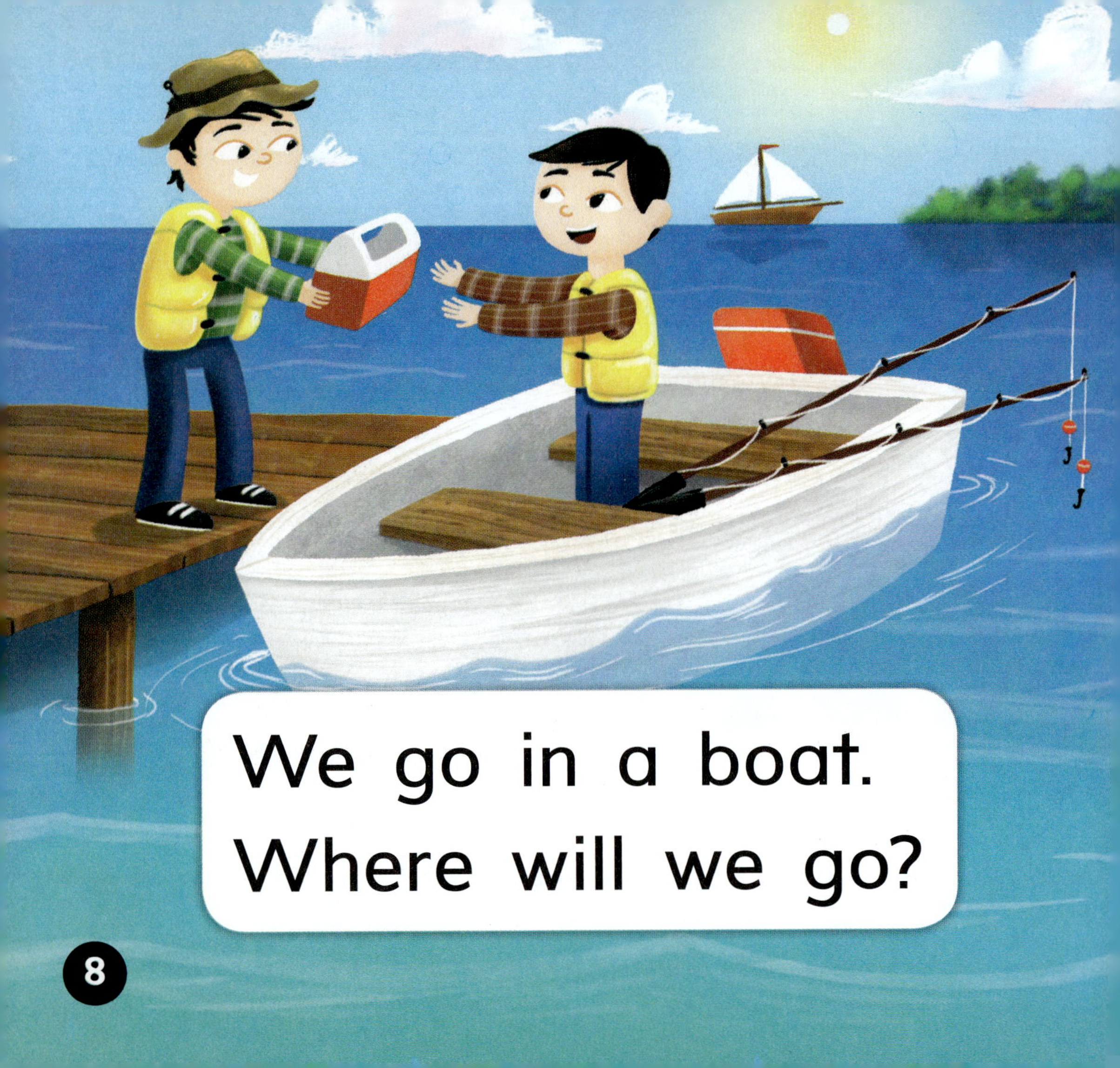

We go in a boat.
Where will we go?